Valentine's Dinner at Wren & Wolf

poems by

Mary Specker Stone

Finishing Line Press
Georgetown, Kentucky

Valentine's Dinner at Wren & Wolf

Publisher: Leah Huete de Maines
Editor: Christen Kincaid
Cover Art: Amy DeCaussin, DeCaussin Studios
Author Photo: Martha Henderson
Cover Design: Elizabeth Maines McCleavy

Order online: www.finishinglinepress.com
         also available on amazon.com

Author inquiries and mail orders:
Finishing Line Press
PO Box 1626
Georgetown, Kentucky 40324
USA

Contents

To Laura, Denise, Kyle, and John
with love

I Am an Empty Bingo Card

I am out of luck and full of possibilities.

I am a sweating tourist in the Sistine Chapel, clutching
my bobble-head Pope.

I am the offspring of a runaway mutt and the bitch next door,
an orphan who can't help but relieve herself on the green shag.

I am land o' lakes, having swallowed Minnesota,
and I am a cave who inhales campfire smoke for breakfast.

I am ice flung from the blade of a windmill,
and I am a cow killed by flying ice.

I am the clearance table with marked-down puzzles
and vinyl totes who whisper *buy me* to passersby.

I am a failed store full of dusty relics. I am the store's
screen door nailed open so I won't rattle in the wind.

I am a private jet with a hired pilot flying
through a moonless sky. I am without a destination.

I am the rotted steeple, resting on the church lawn.
I am the mold growing in the church basement.
I am the church, abandoned.

I am a tectonic plate to stand on, quick,
before it shifts again.

I am unwashed hair, thick with oil and sweat and smoke.
I am burger and fries growing cold on a coffee table.

I am a bee who costs extra to exterminate.

I am first light, hauled out of darkness by four westbound
locomotives, and I'm an oil-slicked pea pod in the chopsticks
of a child who squeals when she sees the train.

I am a last letter written in shaky left-hand script
on grocery store stationery. I lack adequate postage.

I am an apparition, a pre-reality template; no,
I'm a single good eye, tearing at both corners.

Valentine's Dinner at Wren & Wolf

We skirt the intimate, wonder aloud how the shrimp
gets to Phoenix from Rocky Point. Habit, now, to talk
of supply chains, however short. Your confabulation:
a priest who crossed the drug boss in Sonora forced
to broker seafood on the border as penance for mis-
baptizing babies of the corrupt devout. Write a book,
I tell you, I who once half-enjoyed your riffs, hereby
reject our disconnect. We're too old to waste time
and love, look at that gray wolf eyeing us from his
promontory above the hungry stomach of this hip
restaurant, his coat thick, not the least motheaten,
no decommissioned diorama dog, this toothy guy.
He's life-like as you and I, as our own aging canine
whose rear legs splay today as she tries to rise.

Mother's Day, Doorbell

My usual protest well
rehearsed   *why didn't you*
buy them at Safeway,

deliver them yourself,
more sincere. And a kinder
version, though less

sincere   *thank you*
for the flowers. Which
would emerge from my

mouth I couldn't be
assured. But instead
it's Buddha at the door

seated in lotus pose
smack in the center
of the bristled mat

right on the big S.
Thus disarmed I plant
a most sincere kiss

on my foolish husband's lips
and place the serene one
in the shade of a young

hibiscus not yet in bloom.
Tiny grains of nursery soil
rest in his upturned hands,

his nondescript stone
substance surprisingly
soft, already eroding.

The Bride

What is a vow, if not
a warranty? She expects
unlimited parts and labor for one
hundred thousand miles, yet

so much can go wrong—
consider the switches alone,
millions of tiny binaries,
all those zeroes and ones.

She loves the shine of this one's
honeymoon car, dentless,
lacquered satin white, starved
for white, bone china white,

she needs to believe in him.
*Zero is an invention
of the Indians,* he explains
as he peels her gown away.
She doesn't even ask,
which Indians?

Petrichor

The smell of rain after
a long, dry spell, blood

from stone, squeezing tight
to get what a thing can't

give, until suddenly it yields
more than you sought when

you snatched it, so desperate
you'd have murdered for beauty

or rain. The love is worth it,
when the violence stops.

You stay for the romance,
the sweet making up, and

you stay in this desert for rain's
fragrance: rare, honey-green,

coaxed from leaf, not stone.
But, *petrichor*? The chemists'

hybrid word sounds toxic, like
the perfume of a burning world.

Ode to Bottled Water

Oh water-in-a-bottle, how we thirst
for the uncontaminated everlasting,

for the pure, the profitable,
the fountain of beauty and youth.

How we thirst for an existence
unfettered, portable, chilled,

a life we can grasp in one hand.
Oh you who know the thirst

of our lush west, hydrate us
wherever we may go: to the spa

or the jungle, the desert or the ocean,
to the middle of the ocean,

where your crystalline vessels
swirl, majestic, in a conjured

reef twice the size of Texas.
There, you are robed in sunlight,

bejeweled with the language
of emerald and aquamarine.

You, who are condemned
and drunk with praise

in the same measure, save us
from what's on tap.

Playing War

Her big brothers hand
down an army set.
You'd think she'd
know how to play

war, watching
body counts
on Walter Cronkite
over dinner every night,

but she's a doll girl.
She gives her best friend
the green soldiers
and she takes

the blue ones,
and on a blanket
under the plum tree
they know enough

to set the little
plastic warriors
on opposing sides,
but they know better

how to focus
on accessories—
guns, cannons, helmets,
tanks, ammo belts—

and the uniforms
and the nursing
of the wounded
and the cleaning up.

Overlook the Zebra Rug

the pool table in the living room, the sequined
tube top and sparkling blue eyeshadow
on James' mom, a professional pool player.
Don't judge, my mantra since moving here.
Boob jobs, glitter t-shirts, liberal-bashing,
I can overlook lots of Scottsdale mom traits.

I scoop up my son from his play date,
treat him to a Chinese dinner. Over egg rolls
he tells me about the gun, how James took it
out of the master bedroom nightstand, let him
hold it, and how the father then fired the gun
twice at the ceiling to prove it wasn't loaded.

Before I Knew Sin

I learned to ski on the filthy Mississippi,
jammed my feet into stiff rubber bindings,
quick, before the current could slam me
face-first into a red buoy (*red right return,*
I memorized, for the day I would be old
enough to drive the boat), and was lifted
by the gunning outboard motor to glide
on calm sheen above the leeches, mud
and catfish, cattle carcasses and blacksnakes,
unaware of what lay beneath the surface
as I cut away from the looming coal barge
that would suck me under if I skied too close,
and all night long strings of barges slid around
the river's bend, their wakes lapping at
the sandbar where I lay awake, imagining
the river life, its destinations, Memphis
or New Orleans, where I would surely sin,
show my tits, drink hurricanes, partake
of the religion, dark and carnal, catholic
as the river, which drank blood from every
slaughterhouse in the upper Midwest
and washed the sins of Lutherans and heathens
down its vast open sewer to the delta far away,
and when I finished my run, I sank into the thick,
fast water and waited for the boat to circle back,
current sweeping me downriver as I peeled
off skis, handed them up, then hoisted myself,
marked with a waterline of greasy sludge.

A Borrowed Boat

I'd absorbed sailing's essence from my father,
so I thought, though he never handed me the tiller.
Tanned teenage legs glistening with lake spray,
I rode along. arching my body windward when
his boat heeled. I believed I was leveling the craft,
unconscious of the helmsman's full control. This
afternoon, I take you sailing in a borrowed boat
on a Sierra lake. Breeze steady, the occasional gust.
I tack along my mind's lines, believing I can sail
by intuition. My tarot phase, I'm learning to read
non-logical signs, not the wind or a boat's behavior.
These requires the analytic mind I've set aside.
My sudden jibe almost knocks you out.
You duck the slashing boom just in time.

On the Eve of Your Son's Court Appearance

He may be guilty, or he may not.
Possibly, he snapped, you think,

as you snapped at him when he was little.
Is it possible you are guilty now,

you, who taught him to snap his little shirt,
who snapped at him on more than one occasion?

A little snapping, or a lot, it all adds up
by the time a son becomes a man,

a man who may be guilty or may not.
Be sure to wear a clean shirt, you think

(but you don't dare say this aloud),
and don't forget to shave.

When a son becomes a man,
a mother dare not snap advice at him.

Snap out of it, you tell yourself.
He's the one who will appear in court tomorrow.

He may be guilty, or he may not.
Perhaps he wasn't thinking,

or it's possible he just plain snapped.
Sometimes, a little snap is all it takes.

You, who taught him to snap his little shirt,
who snapped at him when he was little,

you may indict yourself as guilty now, but
he's the man who will appear in court tomorrow.

Burr Trail

Whole, for now: sinew, muscle, teeth, brain,
bone. Beef, but not yet beef, reluctant to be

herded from green pasture to an even
lusher place, or perhaps a loading chute.

Horse-mounted cowhands whistle and shout,
push sixty beeves up the narrow highway

where our car is stopped, cattle streaming past
both sides. Huge bovine eye glares into my window:

who are you, pitiless human, with your menu
of meat, who sent your teenage son out here

with only a down bag, parka, tarp, socks, boots? Snow,
cold, rain, lions, lightning: you're lucky he survived.

One boy in his wilderness group didn't. That
spring, did he become more docile, hoofing it?

No Thoroughfare Canyon

time and distance fall away
my impulse is to fill myself with river rock
to lay down in the velvet-silted streambed
placental with autumn's decomposing leaves

my impulse is to fill myself with river rock
to become one with this red canyon's stream
placental with autumn's decomposing leaves
ruffling in sluggish current

to become one with this red canyon's stream
spill a two-note chord over boulders
ruffle in sluggish current
reverberate in the pool below

spilling a two-note chord over boulders
solitude is mine by default
reverberating in the pool below
in this canyon with no thoroughfare

solitude is mine by default
to lay down in the velvet-silted streambed
in this canyon with no thoroughfare
time and distance fall away

Herbert

He was a kettle of popcorn,
a dog-eared map of Missouri,
an Evinrude motor spitting oil into rainbows,
a self-taught sailor on a man-made lake,
a lawn-mowing, snow-shoveling,
foxtrot-dancing, fix-it man,
a dinner at six man.

He was a highball and a bowling ball,
an Old Milwaukee and peanut butter on toast,
a slide rule and a T-square,
a blue-eyed, left-handed slice of ham
so thin you could see right through him,
a son of the Great Depression,
a bowl of dust.

He was Dean Martin and Walter Cronkite,
a white collar walking the construction site.
He was just a man trying to get it right.

He was a chair and a magazine,
a strict routine:
walk two laps, bike four miles,
take the blue pill, then the red pill.

He was a late-blooming ladies' man,
a romance novel with a full head of hair.
He was heartbreak and heart repair.

In the driver's seat of an automobile,
always almost new, he was the compass
pointing west, sunglasses clipped on hornrims,
a thermos full of coffee making good time,
always almost sure he knew exactly
where he was going.

My Father Loved a Dam

The sun shines just long enough
to get him buried, on high ground
overlooking the Missouri River

near his mother, whom he loved,
and his father, whom he didn't,
in a different town altogether

than my mother, his ex-wife,
whose welfare I protect better
in death than I could in life.

Difficult to cross the highway
to the golf course for lunch,
gravel truck traffic thick in both

directions, hauling raw sand east
to shoveling scouts and guardsmen,
and sandbags west to residents

of Pierre, who fortify their town
against the flood, now in progress.
Our little funeral party, grown

children of the just-interred
construction engineer, hurry
from lunch to Oahe dam,

its reservoir near to overtopping,
its five massive release gates,
just this morning, opened wide.

We watch the cataracts boil
downriver, a fitting committal for
a man who lived to bend nature.

On Forgiveness

He can hear the subtlest grace notes of snow falling on snow,
the yellow noise of termites digesting downed wood,

the carbon glide of trains rolling on night tracks
miles away, their whistles silenced by the town council.

He listens now for the melting of my resentment.
Only he knows how this will sound, maybe a drip,

drip like the icicles hanging from our eaves,
which refreeze every night and melt a bit every day.

Or maybe it will sound like baking cookies, the clatter
of beaters as they cream solid shortening with sugar, eggs.

My mother's resentment was like that, a baking sort,
cheesecake made to satisfy her own sweet tooth,

a resentment loved for its own sake. Soundless, maybe
my melting will be so slow, occur over so many years

that he won't hear a thing. Or maybe he'll notice a pause
I take one day before saying something awful, a pause

during which less harsh language has a chance to find itself
forming between my incisors. A prayer to want to forgive,

a prayer to forgive my unforgiveness, I have little use for these,
I tell a well-meaning friend, even as my husband ascends

the roof to place electric cables. He aims to melt the ice dams
that cause our roof to leak. And to prevent more ice forming.

Surgery Consult

What's to become of the nipple?
I ask it straight out.

My left index finger searches the bony edge
of my eye socket, traces its mortal perimeter.

The surgeon tells me he took first runner-up
in the hospital's pumpkin-carving contest,

believes he should have won. How is a breast
like a pumpkin? How is it different? The nipple,

he can't know for sure, he says, until he's inside
my breast, where he's already been with needles,

and where others went before, with x-rays and needles.
There will be radiation after, but first, more needles,

more wheelchairs moving my gowned nakedness
down corridors. Dye injections: do lymph nodes

light up? They don't, though they will excise
a few anyway. The nipple? I ask, envisioning

my left breast lop-sided, nipple-less
under spring silks, in my lover's caress.

My breast   my bluish, petaled longing.
A passable facsimile, he promises.

Canyon

It was the death you'd always
thought you wanted: a romantic
suicide, complete with callous
lover, last hike in a red rock canyon
at night, in a blizzard, with a dog.

And brilliantly (your very hope),
the hypothermia.

They found the woman's body
shrouded in fresh snow. The dog
survives.

You so admired her style.
You hated to give up on the idea,
but unwittingly, you had: you let them
take one tumor, then another.

You weren't thinking, were you,
I want my life, my dear, loss-
riddled life.

Round Robin

Her smile, crooked, stroke-damaged, yet still
sweet, a bit coy, devoid of bitterness by now.

Someone has combed her hair and applied
red lipstick. Propped in bed, she wears

a turquoise muumuu, a swatch of which
will one day adorn a quilt called *Milagro*:

a miracle, how her spirit will visit me
in Phoenix as she dies in San Jose.

But today, the last day I will see my mother
alive, chocolate-brown liquid food pulses

from a bag suspended above her bed, through
a tube, into her stomach. The tube, though,

is losing patency: to replace or remove,
my siblings and I were asked to choose.

Today, the feeding machine clicks every minute
or so as I read her the letters from a dozen cousins

and sisters, a round robin begun during the war.
And we compose her news, not much, since

we're omitting the part about her impending
death. I'm not certain she understands. We report

on grandchildren, the kindness of the staff here,
the copious winter rains. Weather is a reliable topic:

when it's fine, you write how you hope it continues,
when it's bad, how you pray it improves.

Burning

Whenever I make chili, I use whatever I find
in the refrigerator. Today, two serrano chilies,

thirty little garden tomatillos, and grass-fed
beef that's too tough for any purpose but

slow-cooking in a chili. I slice the serranos
lengthwise with my largest chef's knife,

scrape out all the tiny seeds and membranes
with my index fingernail, and chop them small,

not to a mince, but who knows where the line is?
Boiling water loosens tomatillos' paper wrappers,

allows me to easily peel and halve them. My fingers,
not yet burning, I chop an onion, smash a few small

garlic cloves, cut open the package of beef, add
all these to the sauté pan. Roe v Wade has been

overturned. Liberty, as in, history of. Herstory,
the proper term, the one we used at the feminist clinic.

Yes, I'm thinking about the late right to abortion
as I cook this meal, and my fingers begin to burn.

More burning as I wash the dishes. The more water,
the more burn. That's how capsaicin infuses the flesh.

I might have worn latex gloves to handle the serranos,
but I wanted to feel the chilies' crisp greenness

with my unprotected hands, and now, an hour later,
I can barely grip the pen for the burning.

Endarkment

—an anagram poem

I lie naked
in ardent dark,
in a rented
room named
Night's Meander.

Sleep, I dare
you, Dream,
entreat you: enter,

remake, retake,
tend, tame, amend
me. Dark Mater,

I keen
for this night's end.
Amen

To End the River

Weary of spring floods and summer drought,
we take control, ending the river abruptly.

I drink a glass of water, plug in my hair dryer,
think little of it, how the river, having tumbled

through its deep, coppery gorge, placid reservoirs,
and brief home stretch nestled between narrow

bands of cottonwood trees blushed pale yellow
this early December day, just ceases to be.

A diversion dam squeezes the entire Salt River
into two puny canals and a spine of power poles

cascading down to Phoenix. Happy birthday,
my ex-husband tells me on the phone.

Our daughter is turning forty; he wants to give her
something fine, lasting, a pen, he thinks, but Saks

has no such pens. They float offshore, encased
in velvet bags, bejeweled boxes, in a container,

on a ship awaiting a berth and all the hands
and motors and grease required to transport them

to their final destination. Ephemerals, the best
ideas I have for him: a creek that comes and goes,

or flowers in full bloom. Deliver them in person.
If you give her a river, make sure it flows to the sea.

A Birth

Following tail lights
across the dark Mojave,
half-moon above,

we race a baby west.
Overtake one silver trailer,
then the next truck looms.

Text: an epidural.
Text: my ex has arrived,
cat-naps in his Lexus.

*

How can you be grandma
and not be married to grandpa?
At age six, she will grill me.

*

Flying J's a bright oasis.
Fuel up, cross the river,
one state becomes another.

L.A.'s haze at three a.m.,
son-in-law's nervous stubble,
daughter's pained half-smile.

*

How do people fall in love?
In the same precocious chat,
this too, she will ask.

*

Waiting room, vinyl chairs,
sunrise, and a nurse:
born, a curious baby girl.

My dear, sundered daughter
weighs this bewilderment,
and unsmiling, sniffs it.

*

How do people stay in love?
Sweetheart, I'm no expert,
let's ask your mom & dad.

Lesson After Trying Very Hard

Love cannot be forced,
must be allowed to flow
outward over rocky shelves

and pour down, frothing
like worshippers at a tent revival,
mouths flooded with spirit

or like the Benedictine sister
opening to Jesus, her psalms,
chanted over hours, days, and years

wearing away her willfulness,
or lovers—I've seen them—
pulsing in each other's breasts

or the lady cultivating roses:
feeding, watering, pruning
back the innermost thorns

tending so gently
each bloom
as it comes forth.

An Hour North

1.

Ashdod welcomes us with fireworks in blue sky,
laser streaks of orange light, blooms of smoke,
sirens. I'm always on deck to watch our ship's
comings and goings, but today, I can't name what
I'm seeing: the ship, nosing to dock, and suddenly,
not. It pivots, hastens out to sea. My husband's
in the shower. *Tracers*, I yell to him, reaching for
a TV term, the wrong one. These are rockets.
All day, sailing north, Israel's coast is violet haze.
I can just make out the skyline as we sail past Tel Aviv.

2.

The train, a puzzle to us. We almost miss it, waiting
in the Portland station to be called. You offer me
the window; my claustrophobia always needs a view.
This pane unwashed, encrusted with salt, rain, dust;
its patina, a mirror. First, I'm blinded by glare, then
catch a glimpse of steeple, station, bog. Each bog,
a ghost-forest, trees salt-poisoned by the rising sea.
Inebriated Red Sox fans carom up and down the aisle
to the bar car. The train shudders to a stop an hour north
of Boston. "We've hit a deer!" one drunk hollers.

3.

In the mural, a figure who resembles Dad as he looked
in 1935, shirtless and skinny, belt cinched to hold up
cheap pants. Bent to the jackhammer, chiseling sandstone
where a dam will rise. He never worked for the WPA,
but he would have, given the chance. Why do I miss him
more than the others? Today's autumn air is cool and still;
the summer sun stung, but now it's lost its stinger. Did he
ever buy himself nice pants? He could have, later on.
His second wife, the elegant one from Pasadena: I bet
she made him buy nice pants, and a dinner jacket, too.

4.
I buy three-dollar eclipse glasses, red, white & blue,
with an eagle, serious, but not fierce. From the parking lot
of the Speedway Fuel and Convenience store in Gallup, NM,
I watch the moon slide into the center of the sun, and then,
snap: a perfect gold ring. You'll have to take my word for it.
No camera, no tripod or solar filter, and my retinas, too delicate
to mess with sun in cellphone's lens. The moon slides on.
I gaze through my safety glasses till my neck aches.
A few pickup trucks pull in for lotto tickets, 12-packs.
Most locals stay indoors, observing the death of the sun.

5.
A mockingbird is singing in the chimney,
its song, spring-crisp, yellow as the blooms on
the paloverde trees. Amplified, pouring
from the fireplace into the room where
I love you. In and out of this room we amble.
At times, all I hear is birdsong. Other times, none at all.
Was it you who showed me how to reach up the flue,
open the damper, admit more song?
Was it me who said, enough music
today: I want to hear you.

Afternoon at La Posada

Trains stop in Winslow
to reconfigure, and we do, too,
in the Betty Grable room

where blinds close out
late afternoon's glare
and the air conditioner purrs.

Your face, my legs, fresh-
shaven. Misshapen, my left
breast, and smaller now.

Sapphire, our rings,
our gin. Outside
the wind shakes pollen

from the hollyhocks
and lofts cottonwoods'
seed-down. An eastbound

freight rattles past,
while on a siding
a whole new train

is composed. as boxcar
by graffitied boxcar
is coupled into place.

October

If I think too much about this
birch, its claw-like limbs poised

in black and white relief against
the bay, it will cease resembling

a tree, such is the power of my mind
to destroy a moment's beauty.

I used to help my children
find hidden pictures in the trees:

always a flute, a broom, a candle.
In a tree on West 95th, the face of Jesus.

What hides in this birch? Look,
my dears, how its last yellow leaves

cling to the uppermost twigs where
you'd think they'd blow off first.

Most tenacious, those places
at the very edges of a creature.

Theology of a Boy Soprano

On a hidden riser, he stands tall
enough to clear the lectern,
his knotted black tie, stark

against an ill-fitting white shirt.
Above him, checkered blocks of shadow
and light kaleidoscope on sanctuary's wall

as sunlight's angle grows more acute.
It is late November. We are deep
into this requiem for the living,

dabbing eyes, sorry to be carrying on.
Voice uncertain, the boy begins his solo,
Agnus Dei, lamb of god: *who takes away*

the sins of the world? Light and shadow
kiss his cowlicked head as we search
the libretto for the missing question mark.

Acknowledgments

"Theology of a Boy Soprano" was inspired by Dan Forrest's "Requiem for the Living," as performed by the Saint Barnabas Episcopal Church choir, soloists, and orchestra, November, 2022, in Scottsdale, Arizona.

With gratitude to the following publications, where versions of these poems appeared:
Gila River Review: "Ode to Bottled Water"
Gleam: Journal of the Cadralor: "An Hour North"
Gyroscope Review: "Valentine's Dinner at Wren & Wolf;" "Mother's Day, Doorbell;" "I Am an Empty Bingo Card"
Image Journal: "Before I Knew Sin"
New Verse News: "Burning"
Paradise Review: "On Forgiveness"
Presence: an International Journal of Spiritual Direction: "Endarkment"
Sheila-Na-Gig Online: "A Birth"

Thank you to the Community of Writers in Phoenix, Arizona, for your friendship, inspiration, support, and critique. And to Tina Barry, for helping me wrangle an early draft of this manuscript. Thanks also to Amy DeCaussin for your skill, patience, and creativity, and to Martha Henderson for your photography talent and infectious spirit. David Watts and Lois Roma-Deeley, thank you for offering me encouragement and early publishing opportunities. And for nurturing my craft and confidence, deep bows to the Napa Valley Writers Conference and its stellar faculty.

I am immensely grateful to my family: my grandchildren, who remind me to pay close attention to small things; and my children, for becoming the beautiful, gifted, compassionate people you are. Thanks also to my late poet-genealogist-cousin, Betty Nicholas Bowers, who introduced me to the poetic tradition in my maternal family line. And special thanks to my husband John, who is my valentine.

After a long career as a biomedical writer in the pharmaceutical and medical diagnostics industries, **Mary Specker Stone** pursued graduate studies in medical rhetoric, earning her M.A. from Northern Arizona University. She turned to poetry during her years as a college English instructor and grant writer, publishing poems in various journals including *Image Journal; The Healing Art of Writing, vol. 1; New Verse News; Gyroscope Review; Gleam; Sheila-Na-Gig Online;* and *Presence.* Now a certified spiritual director, she lives in the Phoenix area, where she leads poetry salons and serves as a spiritual companion to writers, artists, and people in recovery.